31 Days
with God
FOR GRADS

BARBOUR
PUBLISHING

Published by Barbour Publishing, Inc., P.O. Box 719, Uhrichsville, Ohio 44683, www.barbourbooks.com

Our mission is to publish and distribute inspirational products offering exceptional value and biblical encouragement to the masses.

ecpa Member of the
Evangelical Christian
Publishers Association

Printed in the United States of America.

Seeking the Truth

*Avoid godless, foolish discussions with those
who oppose you with their so-called knowledge.*
1 Timothy 6:20 NLT

Young adulthood is the time to decide what you do and do not believe to be true. It's a time to question everything, reject some old things, and embrace some new things. It's a time that makes parents worry, because they know you will be looking critically at their beliefs, too.

You have to do this. You can't blindly accept everything you hear. You have to make your own decisions and be prepared to live with them, or you'll be a wishy-washy nobody.

You also have to learn discernment. That's what Paul was warning Timothy about. Some positions must be taken on faith. All the talk in the world can't prove the unprovable, so look at everything carefully before you decide to embrace a stand—but realize that some things just have to be accepted on faith, not facts.

Father, no one seems to agree on anything, including faith. Give me discernment and the courage to stand by my beliefs, even if I can't prove they are correct.

We know the truth not only by
the reason but also by the heart.
BLAISE PASCAL

REST FOR THE WEARY

Then I heard the voice of the Lord saying,
"Whom shall I send? And who will go for us?"
And I said, "Here am I. Send me!"
ISAIAH 6:8

Ever wish that you could rewrite that verse to say, "Here am I. Send someone else"? When you feel overloaded spiritually, even though you'd like to comply, opening yourself to full obedience to God is hard.

Maybe, you worry, *if I give Him free rein, He'll send me to Tombouctou* (or wherever your least-favorite place in the world is). *How could I ever cope with that?* you wonder.

If you're feeling overloaded, take your burden to God and confess that you've been hanging on to it. Then drop it in His hands and run! Don't stick around to pull it back out of the hands of the great burden-lifter.

Then let Him lead you as you make decisions about ministries with which you're over involved, family problems that someone else needs to handle, or commitments you may not need to take on. Pledge yourself to obedience and walk in your new freedom. Don't let that old burden trap you again!

Send me, Lord, wherever You want me to go. I know You'll give me the strength I need.

Faith never knows where it is being led, but it loves and knows the One who is leading.

OSWALD CHAMBERS

LOOKING FOR DIRECTION

"For I know the plans I have for you," says the LORD.
"They are plans for good and not for disaster,
to give you a future and a hope."
JEREMIAH 29:11 NLT

We all have plans for our future, even if they're a little vague. We know whether we want to marry and have children, places we want to go, and things we hope to accomplish. Most of us are realistic about our plans, knowing some will work out and some won't. We also know our plans will change from year to year as we mature and see more of the world.

What we don't like is to have our plans blown out of the water and to have our lives take a sudden change of direction. There's nothing more frightening than losing the anchor that's been holding our life in place and being forced to start over again.

Fortunately, some of these disasters turn out to be blessings. Even when we have no idea which way to turn, the Lord knows where we're going and will keep us on the right path, even if the trip's a little bumpy.

Father, when my life suddenly turns upside down, I will trust in You to lead me in the right direction.

Walk boldly and wisely. . . . There is a hand above that will help you on.

PHILIP JAMES BAILEY

TAKING TIME TO PRAY

*But when you pray, go into your room, close the
door and pray to your Father, who is unseen.*
MATTHEW 6:6

Time got away from Amy that morning, and prayer seemed to be out of the question. Jumping in her car, she decided, *I'll just pray while I drive.*

As she started off, so did her prayer, but soon she got caught in traffic. Faced with the choice of having an accident or praying, she kept her mind on the road. Past the traffic, Amy turned again to prayer, only to lose track once more when she saw a sale sign on one of her favorite stores.

Sure, you can pray while you drive—maybe you should sometimes—but if that's the only time you spend with God, you won't be giving Him your best. After all, two seconds of prayer here and a minute there can't compete with solid time when God can answer you.

If you only talked to your friends while you drove, you couldn't give them your full attention, and your communication would get mixed up. It's the same with God.

Lord, I know I can pray when I drive, but there are too many distractions to make it my prayer room. My life includes time to spend with You. Show me when it is.

Is prayer your steering wheel
or your spare tire?
CORRIE TEN BOOM

"PRETTY IS AS PRETTY DOES"

*"Stop judging by mere appearances,
and make a right judgment."*
JOHN 7:24

Our whole country is caught up in appearance today, almost to the point of making it an idol. We are consumed by the desire to be thin, to be beautiful, to dress with flair and style. All of these may be perfectly legitimate personal goals, but we can all too easily pervert them, try to impose them on others, and then judge everyone as unworthy who doesn't measure up.

Today the fit mock those who puff their way up the stairs. The beautiful recommend nose jobs. The tall look down on the small; those who look as if they need a good sandwich feel superior to those who have obviously had too many.

Jesus tells us to look beyond the surface—to judge actions, not appearances. We have no right to make our personal preferences the basis for judging the worthiness of others.

Father, just as I don't want to be judged by my acceptance of some popular trend, neither do I want to judge others by my own personal preferences. Keep me sensitive to the feelings of others and help me see the true person beyond the surface.

∞

I don't like that man.
I must get to know him better.
ABRAHAM LINCOLN

Heading for Holiness

*Let us purify ourselves from everything that
contaminates body and spirit, perfecting
holiness out of reverence for God.*
2 Corinthians 7:1

Unless you plan to live the life of a hermit, this verse is going to give you problems. We live in a thoroughly contaminated world where it's difficult to be even a little holy, let alone perfectly holy.

Start with the most important fact, though: Your sins have already been forgiven. How do you thank someone for saving your life now and forever? By trying to be what He wants you to be. No, you are not going to do it perfectly. Yes, you will still sin. But you will also steer clear of situations that God disapproves of. You will treat your body as the holy temple of God, who lives in you, and you will treat others the way you want to be treated. It's a start, anyway, and this is one case where good intentions do count.

*Father, I can never live my life in total holiness,
but I can show my thankfulness and reverence
for You in many ways. Help me live my life in a
way that will reflect Your glory and mercy and
eternal love.*

∽

How little people know who think
that holiness is dull. When one meets
the real thing, it is irresistible.
C. S. LEWIS

BE A BLESSING

Suppose a brother or sister is without clothes and daily food. If one of you says to him, "Go, I wish you well; keep warm and well fed," but does nothing about his physical needs, what good is it?
JAMES 2:15–16

Billions of dollars are spent in America every year on movies and other forms of entertainment. Meanwhile, the view in other areas of America is hardly "entertaining." Churches struggle financially, and some needy families only get help when their stories reach the six o'clock news. Is it any surprise our nation is in trouble?

If we gave as generously to God as we do to our entertainment, imagine the people who could be helped. Churches could expand ministries to the inner city and support ministries all over the world. There'd be enough money to help a struggling family get back on its feet.

There are even ways to help that don't require money. Recycle. Volunteer with a local charity or school. Donate clothes you don't need. These efforts make a big difference to the lives that are affected.

The blessings that come with generous giving can hardly be imagined. Let's start the blessings today.

Lord, make me understand what I can and cannot do to help others in the world today. Show me the small actions I can take that will make a difference.

∞

The manner of giving shows the character of the giver more than the gift itself.
JOHANN KASPAR LAVATER

MODEL OBEDIENCE

*In everything that he undertook in the service
of God's temple and in obedience to the law and
the commands, he sought his God and worked
wholeheartedly. And so he prospered.*
2 CHRONICLES 31:21

King Hezekiah was totally committed to the service of God, seeking His will and working wholeheartedly. As a result, he prospered.

The Bible doesn't say that Hezekiah had an easy time of it. If you read his whole story, you'll see he worked harder than today's corporate leaders ever do. There must have been days when he was sick of all the organizing, rebuilding, defending, and other chores that fall on a king. He'd solve one problem only to have six others appear. Hezekiah wasn't perfect, either. He and the whole kingdom were punished for their pride when Hezekiah neglected to give God the glory for a miracle.

He must have been a wise man to rule successfully for twenty-nine years. But remember, Hezekiah was twenty-five when he became king! What would happen if we committed our lives to God and wholeheartedly followed His will?

Lord, teach me to seek Your will with all my heart, and do it with the wisdom and enthusiasm of Hezekiah, the young king who was rewarded for his faithfulness.

∽

On board iron vessels it is a common thing to see a compass placed aloft, to be as much away from the cause of aberration as possible: a wise hint to us to elevate our affections and desires. The nearer to God, the less swayed by worldly influences.

CHARLES SPURGEON

TURNING TIME

*And the sun stood still, and the moon stayed, until the
people had avenged themselves upon their enemies. . . .
So the sun stood still in the midst of heaven, and hasted
not to go down about a whole day.*
JOSHUA 10:13 KJV

Amazing—at a time when they needed it, God gave Israel an extra full day of light! The sun and the moon cooperated with humanity's need because God declared it. We can't explain how it happened. Used to the regular rising of the sun and moon, we can't imagine things any other way. It must have also astonished the Amorites, whom Israel was attacking. Instead of getting away under the cover of night, they had to keep fighting.

Now we have an extra day that only comes once every four years. Unlike the Amorites, it's not a total surprise to us. How do we use the extra twenty-four hours?

Every day is important. God doesn't have to stop time to make it so. How will you use today?

Thank You, Lord, for another day to serve You. I want to make the most of it by showing someone Your love.

∾

Place all the hours of this day quite simply at His disposal, and ask Him to make and keep you ready to do just exactly what He appoints.

FRANCES HAVERGAL

REMAINING PURE

God wants you to be holy, so you should keep clear of all sexual sin. Then each of you will control your body and live in holiness and honor—not in lustful passion as the pagans do, in their ignorance of God and his ways.
1 THESSALONIANS 4:3–5 NLT

Avoiding sexual immorality does not come naturally—it has to be learned—and there are very few teachers you can count on today. Society at large is pretty useless, issuing plenty of warnings about disease but little positive, practical advice for those struggling to lead a sanctified life.

So who is available to teach these lessons? The best teacher is God Himself, who can teach you what He expects through the Bible. Use a good concordance to look up verses about sex, love, marriage, and so forth. You can't obey laws you don't know exist, but all the laws are there in the Bible. Besides knowledge, God can give you the strength you will need to control your own body and to live a pure life. Ask for His help when you need it.

Father, thank You for guiding me in all things.
Forgive me when I disappoint You, and give me
the strength I need to please You.

∽

Opportunity may knock only once, but
temptation leans on the doorbell.

AUTHOR UNKNOWN

TELLING TALENTS

One generation will commend your works to another; they will tell of your mighty acts. They will speak of the glorious splendor of your majesty, and I will meditate on your wonderful works.
PSALM 145:4–5

There was no Internet, no instant communication, in the days of David. Most people couldn't read or write. Traditions were taught to the next generation by the older generation through stories, songs, and dances, which were memorable and enjoyable ways to learn. The psalms and hymns of the church not only lifted people's spirits but served as teaching tools.

Perhaps you were not cut out to be a witness. The thought of speaking to another person about your beliefs may scare you into silence. But there are other ways to communicate. Can you tell stories? Can you sing? Can you dance? Can you draw? Faith, and the joy it brings you, can be communicated through many means. Offer God the talents you do have, and He will give you a way to use them.

Father, show me how I can tell others about Your mighty works and pass on the faith I treasure. You know what I am capable of, and I do want to help.

❦

Our gifts and attainments are not only to be light and warmth in our own dwellings, but are also to shine through the windows into the dark night, to guide and cheer bewildered travelers on the road.

Henry Ward Beecher

KNOWING THE REWARDS

*To the man who pleases him, God gives wisdom,
knowledge and happiness, but to the sinner he
gives the task of gathering and storing up wealth
to hand it over to the one who pleases God.*
ECCLESIASTES 2:26

Wisdom, knowledge, and happiness are the rewards of those who please God. These rewards come directly from God, with no one in between. What goes around comes around, and the sinner ends up with nothing. Sometimes life doesn't seem to work this way, but a lot goes on that we don't see, and we have to take the Lord's word for it, because this is a long-term promise.

More importantly, Ecclesiastes 2:26 helps us set our priorities. Our most important task is pleasing God with the way we live. If we do this, the rewards will follow. God Himself will provide us with the wisdom, knowledge, and happiness we need, and financial rewards will follow from them. Sin, on the other hand, has no long-term rewards at all.

Father, I want to please You with my life. If my actions result in rewards, I will be thankful for them, but living my life according to Your wishes is the greatest reward of all.

∽

It is His business to lead, command, impel, send, call, or whatever you want to call it. It is your business to obey, follow, move, respond, or what have you.

JIM ELLIOT

THE LAW VS. GRACE

*Some men came down from Judea to Antioch
and were teaching the brothers: "Unless you
are circumcised, according to the custom taught
by Moses, you cannot be saved."*

ACTS 15:1

People—even some well-meaning Christians—have a hard time accepting grace. They can't believe they don't have to add something to God's work. So they set up rules and regulations: "You have to do *this*, or you aren't a Christian." "You don't really love God unless you do *that*."

The men in this verse were trying to follow the Old Testament Law as well as Jesus. They couldn't accept that His blood had done it all and that, when they accepted Him, their hearts, not their bodies, were circumcised. Many serious Gentile believers who wanted to obey God but feared doing something wrong did what these Judaizers said, unnecessarily. Fear led them into sin.

God doesn't want you to be afraid, to worry if you've dotted all the *i*'s and crossed all the *t*'s that will let you enter heaven. No, He loves you, so He gave you a free gift, no strings attached. Enjoy that gift today.

Thank You, Jesus, for Your grace. You've done everything that had to be done to bring me into heaven. I want to give my life as thanks.

≈

Law tells me how crooked I am;
grace comes along and straightens me out.
D. L. MOODY

THE POWER OF PRAYER

My intercessor is my friend as my eyes pour
out tears to God; on behalf of a man he pleads
with God as a man pleads for his friend.
JOB 16:20–21

How do you pray for others? Is it merely, "Bless John, help Jane"? Imagine yourself in God's shoes, listening to such a shopping list of prayer. Pretty boring, isn't it? Hearing such stuff must be harder for Him than praying it is for us.

God's heart breaks when He thinks of all the blessings we could ask for that He would gladly give. But if He gave what we asked, what would that be? Are we looking for healing, peaceful relationships, conversion, or a thousand other things?

We'll never quite know how prayer works to move God's hand. But through the Spirit, who intercedes for us, we can bring to Him the needs of friends, family, and even Christians who live half a world away. Lives begin to change, and we can praise God for His works.

The Spirit intercedes for you every day. Are you interceding for others, too?

Father God, fill me with Your love for others.
Let my prayer time be a blessing to the world.

∽

Beware in your prayers, above everything
else, of limiting God, not only by unbelief,
but by fancying that you know what He can
do. Expect unexpected things, "above all
that we ask or think." Each time, before you
intercede, be quiet first, and worship God
in His glory. Think of what He can do, and
how He delights to hear the prayers of His
redeemed people. Think of your place and
privilege in Christ, and expect great things!
Andrew Murray

FRIENDLY GOSSIP

A perverse man stirs up dissension,
and a gossip separates close friends.
PROVERBS 16:28

Finding and keeping good friends is hard work. You go through a lot of acquaintances before you find one friend you can trust totally and be honest with—and then you have to work at staying friends with him or her.

One of the best ways to lose a friend is to listen to gossip: "You know what he said about you?" The only proper answer to this question is, "No, and I don't want to hear about it from you." You never know the intentions of a gossip, and it's foolish to listen to one. If you have a problem with a friend, it should stay between the two of you until you work it out. No third party is going to help. Refuse to listen to gossip about a friend if you value the friendship.

Lord, gossip can sometimes be fun, but more often it's dangerous. Give me the good sense to ignore it and deal honestly with my friends in all things.

∽

Whoever keeps an open ear for tattlers will be sure to hear the trumpet of contention.
WILLIAM COWPER

PROVING YOUR WORTH

"Whoever can be trusted with very little can also be trusted with much, and whoever is dishonest with very little will also be dishonest with much."
LUKE 16:10

You're just starting off in your job, and nobody trusts you with very much. You do what you're told, day after day, and it gets pretty boring after awhile. Where's the challenge? What do you have to do before you get to make a few decisions or enjoy some responsibility?

Unfortunately, you have to keep on doing what you're doing—only better. You have to master the boring stuff first—really get it down pat—and be the best "nobody" anyone's ever seen. Don't think people aren't watching, because they are. But even boring work has to be done well, and if you sleepwalk through the day, it will be noticed. However, if you prove yourself trustworthy in this job, a better one will be ahead for you. At the very least, you'll end up with a good reference for your resume.

Father, when my work gets so boring I want to nod off about midafternoon, remind me that I hold the keys to my own success in my own hands. I may be a nobody now, but I won't be for long, with Your help.

❧

I seem to have been led little by little, toward my work; and I believe that the same fact will appear in the life of anyone who will cultivate such powers as God has given him, and then go on, bravely, quietly, but persistently, doing such work as comes to his hands.

FANNY CROSBY

WORRYING—AND CONTENTMENT

*"Who of you by worrying can add
a single hour to his life?"*
MATTHEW 6:27

With a closet full of clothes, we worry about not having "anything" or the "right" thing to wear. With a cupboard full of food, there's still "nothing" to eat. These are minor worries not based on fact, but they continue to nag at us until we go out and buy the "right" clothes or cram the cupboard with enough food to feed a small nation.

Many people have more legitimate worries—actual needs that consume every waking moment in a struggle for survival. What's amazing is that many of these people are still happy, despite their problems. How do they do it? Perhaps they've read a little further in Matthew 6, where Jesus promised, "Seek first his kingdom and his righteousness, and all these things will be given to you as well" (v. 33).

Worry wastes time and produces nothing, while seeking God and His kingdom is always a worthwhile activity that will banish trivial worries and provide us with whatever we need.

Father, I know the rent money will be there when I need it if I concentrate on living righteously and don't let my worries paralyze me. Times may get tough, but I can make it with Your help.

⁓

Seek not great things for yourselves in this world, for if your garments be too long, they will make you stumble; and one staff helps a man in his journey, when many in his hands at once hinders him.

WILLIAM BRIDGE

PREPAREDNESS

And others had trial of cruel mockings and scourgings, yea, moreover of bonds and imprisonment: They were stoned, they were sawn asunder, were tempted, were slain with the sword: they wandered about in sheepskins and goatskins; being destitute, afflicted, tormented; (of whom the world was not worthy).
HEBREWS 11:36–38 KJV

Most of us will never have to face death for our faith, but there are dangers in feeling too safe. For one thing, someone in a safe country never even thinks about martyrdom—personal martyrdom. We aren't prepared for it and have no idea how we would react to that type of danger. What would you do if you had to renounce your faith in order to live? What would you do to keep your children alive? You can't make these decisions wisely and rationally when someone's pointing a gun at your head, and there won't be any chance to change your mind. Think about it now, while there's time—just in case.

Father, I don't even want to think about this happening to me, but give me the strength and the courage to do what I have to do if the time should ever come.

∾

Oh, how much those men are to be valued
who, in the spirit with which the widow
gave up her two mites, have given up
themselves! How their names sparkle!
How rich their very ashes are!
How they will count up in heaven!
EDWIN HUBBELL CHAPIN

HONING OUR HEARING

Whether you turn to the right or to the left,
your ears will hear a voice behind you, saying,
"This is the way; walk in it."
ISAIAH 30:21

God has not left us alone on the earth to struggle through our lives without guidance. Whether we call it God's voice or our own conscience, it is there to help us. We have the freedom to ignore the voice and go our own way. There are no marionette strings attached to us that God to pull to keep us on the path. He will tell us which way to go, but we control our own actions.

The same thing happens to parents who raise their children properly and then can do nothing but watch when something goes wrong and their children turn to drugs or crime. Imagine the pain those parents feel and then multiply it to infinity to begin to understand a fraction of the pain we must cause our heavenly Father.

Don't let the world's uproar drown out the voice you hear behind you. It's the best friend you will ever have.

Father, I want to follow Your path. Help me listen when You guide me in the way I should go.

❦

Conscience is thoroughly well-bred
and soon leaves off talking to those
who do not wish to hear it.

SAMUEL BUTLER

THE RIGHT KIND OF SERVICE

*Therefore all things whatsoever ye would that men
should do to you, do ye so to them: for this
is the law and the prophets.*
MATTHEW 7:12 KJV

Jana sat in the crowded doctor's office, miserable with a head cold and barely paying attention to her surroundings. If only she could get in to see the doctor and get home and to bed!

She barely noticed the grimacing man across from her until another patient told the nurse, "He's in more pain than I am. Please take him first."

Jana admired the woman, but guilt stabbed her heart. *I never realized he was in such pain,* she thought. *If I had, would I have done the same, even though it meant a longer wait?*

Doing good for others—especially those outside our circle of friends—means tuning into their needs. Do we block ourselves behind a pseudospiritual wall and a "don't touch" mentality? Or do we open up to others, talk to hurting people, and offer them Jesus' help?

After all, that's only a small part of what He gave us.

Jesus, reaching out is hard when I get boxed into myself. Open my heart and eyes so I can help others.

∞

The idea that service to God should have only to do with a church altar, singing, reading, sacrifice, and the like is without doubt but the worst trick of the devil. How could the devil have led us more effectively astray than by the narrow conception that service to God takes place only in a church and by the works done therein. . . . The whole world could abound with the services to the Lord, Gottesdienste—not only in churches but also in the home, kitchen, workshop, field.

MARTIN LUTHER

THE MUSIC DEBATE

Worship the LORD with gladness;
come before him with joyful songs.
PSALM 100:2

Some music sounds good to you—and some is just irritating noise. But your "noise" is another person's "sounds good."

Church music is part of the "noise"–"sounds good" debate. If your congregation likes the "oldies and moldies" of Christian music and you like the latest tunes on the Christian music shelves, you may be tempted to hold your ears during services. Worse, those slow, dull songs may lull you to sleep.

Maybe the music you can't stand is favored by your pastor or music leader. Maybe other church members have encouraged the music director to play it. And asking anyone to change the music style could start World War III.

This psalm doesn't mention the kind of music churches should play—it doesn't specify classical, pop, rock music, or even Old Testament–style music. That's because the music itself isn't important— worshipping God is. He deserves our praise, no matter what the song is. A joyful heart can always praise Him.

Whether or not your church is tuned in to your music style, sing with all your heart.

Lord, I want to praise You, not start a war. Thank You for music I enjoy. Let me sing Your praises today.

∞

The only music minister to whom the Lord will say, "Well done, thou good and faithful servant," is the one whose life proves what their lyrics are saying, and to whom music is the least important part of their life. Glorifying the only worthy One has to be a minister's most important goal!

KEITH GREEN

UNDER COVER

"You have not lied to men but to God."
ACTS 5:4

Okay, so maybe you aren't like Ananias. You've never lied about how much money you had to give. But are you honest with God?

That's tough. After all, to be totally honest with God means letting Him inside those deep, dark places no one else knows about. The date that was going so well, until. . . Your real thoughts about that coworker. . . The way you really feel about things in His Word.

We'd like to hide from God. Our messy lives just don't seem good enough for Him. The problem is, until we open up to Him, we'll never change. God doesn't barge into our hearts, ferreting out sin. Instead, He woos us, shows us the right path, and invites us to give up those dark holes in our lives.

If we don't, we may not get suddenly wiped out, like Ananias, but a slow spiritual death creeps into our lives. Is it creeping into your life?

Lord, it's hard to be honest with someone as holy as You. But I want to be like You in this, too. Cleanse my heart.

❧

Character is what you are in the dark.
D. L. MOODY

TRUSTING HIM

He is the Rock, his work is perfect: for all
his ways are judgment: a God of truth
and without iniquity, just and right is he.
DEUTERONOMY 32:4 KJV

Wise men and women have wrestled with this verse for centuries, so it's not unusual for the average person to ask the obvious question: If God is just, why isn't His world? Why don't the good prosper and the evil fail? Why do starvation and genocide still rage today?

One obvious answer is that God is working with flawed materials—us. Over the course of history, we've changed the world, but not always for the better. He gave us dominion over the earth, and our sin has corrupted a perfectly just situation.

Maybe the best answer to the just-God/unjust-world problem is to admit that we simply don't know what's going on. We're not seeing the whole picture. Even if we could, we probably wouldn't understand it. Some things we just have to take on faith. God is still in the world, doing what only He can do.

Father, I place my life in Your hands, certain that all things work according to Your will, whether I understand or not.

❧

Never be afraid to trust an unknown
future to a known God.

CORRIE TEN BOOM

FAIR-WEATHER FRIENDS

*And as they sat and did eat, Jesus said, Verily I say unto
you, One of you which eateth with me shall betray me.
And they began to be sorrowful, and to say unto him
one by one, Is it I? and another said, Is it I?*
MARK 14:18–19 KJV

Just the kind of firm believers you'd like to have following you if you were about to face the cross, right? Twelve men who aren't even sure of their own hearts! Told that one would betray Jesus, for a single, honest moment, not one disciple—not even brash Peter—guaranteed he would never give in.

But Jesus used these less-than-confident men precisely because they recognized their own weakness. God doesn't look for self-sufficient disciples who never err. He looks for those who know they are weak and know whom to turn to—Jesus.

If you're facing trouble and feel you lack the strength to stand firm, don't waste your time worrying; turn to Jesus instead. You're in exactly the right place.

Lord Jesus, I'm so weak that sometimes I don't even realize it. When I face a cross, I can trust only in You.

⁂

So let it be in God's own might
We gird us for the coming fight,
And, strong in Him whose cause is ours
In conflict with unholy powers,
We grasp the weapons he has given,—
The Light, and Truth, and Love of Heaven.

JOHN GREENLEAF WHITTIER

BUILDING UP

Then I said to them, "You see the trouble we are in:
Jerusalem lies in ruins, and its gates have been burned
with fire. Come, let us rebuild the wall of Jerusalem,
and we will no longer be in disgrace."
NEHEMIAH 2:17

Overcome with discouragement, the Jews who had returned to Jerusalem from exile huddled in a city open to invaders. Broken walls surrounded what was left of the city, and even its gates were burned. But no one started a citywide rebuilding project.

When Nehemiah heard of the situation, instead of hunkering down in fear, he got permission to rebuild the walls. He traveled to Jerusalem, inspected the site, and confronted the people. Encouragement and a plan were all the people needed—and Nehemiah gave them both.

Every Christian needs lifting up. When job hunting gets you down, it's great to have someone show you the ropes and say something heartening. If you're struggling with sin, a seasoned Christian can share how he or she overcame the same temptation.

Don't let discouragement get the best of you. Reach out for help!

When I feel lower than a snake, Lord, it's hard to tell others. Help me reach out for help.

∞

There are high spots in all of our lives, and most of them have come about through encouragement from someone else.
GEORGE MATTHEW ADAMS

DEALING WITH ANGER

A quick-tempered man does foolish things.
PROVERBS 14:17

People handle anger in various ways. Some manage to push it down and continue as if they never felt it (probably giving themselves ulcers in the process). Others kick chairs in private but soon come to terms with their anger. Still others blow up and immediately feel better. We tend to react to anger the same way our parents did.

In the same way, we all have different boiling points. It takes a lot to get some people angry, while others erupt at the slightest provocation.

However you react to anger, you need to maintain control. Anger makes us stupid. We do and say things we would never do under normal circumstances, starting fistfights or saying words we can never take back.

When anger takes over, get away if you can't control your emotions. Go hide out in the rest room, if necessary. Shut a door behind you until you are back in control. A real man does not hit. A strong woman asserts control over herself, not over others.

Father, when I want to strike out in anger, whether verbally or physically, give me the self-control I need to avoid doing anything stupid.

The best time for you to hold
your tongue is the time you feel
you must say something or bust.
JOSH BILLINGS

PLAYING THE FOOL

The fool says in his heart, "There is no God."
They are corrupt, their deeds are vile;
there is no one who does good.
PSALM 14:1

We may call ourselves a fool when we spill milk or forget to pick something up at the store. We should have known better, but we just weren't paying attention. Yet this sort of carelessness isn't the kind of foolishness God talks about in His Word. When God calls someone a fool, He's very serious. In scripture, fools are those who don't believe in Him.

To God, anyone who ignores the obvious messages He's given the world is missing more than mental focus. Real foolish thinking—such as self-centeredness and disregard for right—steeps a person in wickedness. Apart from God, no one does good.

We don't need to be hard on ourselves when we forget to pick up bread at the grocery store, but we do need to be careful that we don't emulate the works of the truly foolish—those who don't believe God even exists.

Lord, any goodness I do comes from You. When others deny You, I want to stand firm in faith instead of acting as if You don't exist.

❧

As a vessel is known by the sound,
whether it be cracked or not;
so men are proved, by their speeches,
whether they be wise or foolish.

DEMOSTHENES

UNDER THE INFLUENCE

Do not be misled: "Bad company corrupts good character."
1 CORINTHIANS 15:33

The world is full of "bad company" we can't avoid. The best we can do is recognize them for what they are and not let them influence our personal lives.

We do have a voice concerning who we choose to hang around with, but since it takes time to really know a person, we also make mistakes. Sometimes we become friends with someone who is fun to be with, who eases our loneliness—but we soon discover we really don't like some of the things going on. We want to break off the relationship, but that's hard. "Maybe it's not really all that serious." "Maybe I can change him."

It's at this point, when we begin rationalizing insupportable behavior, that our good character becomes corrupted. We overlook one flaw after another until we can no longer say, "This is wrong. I can't do this." A corrupt person is one who can't see the difference between good and bad.

Father, give me the wisdom to choose my friends carefully, and when I make a mistake, give me the courage to break off the relationship before I begin to think and act like a corrupt person myself.

❧

No man is the whole of himself;
his friends are the rest of him.

HARRY EMERSON FOSDICK

DANGEROUS DABBLING

*I will cut off. . .them that worship
the host of heaven upon the housetops.*
ZEPHANIAH 1:4-5 KJV

B ut the occult is dangerous," Brendan warned his church group. "Why—"

Another group member quickly cut him off, pooh-poohing his words. Some in the study didn't want to admit that reading a horoscope was unbiblical.

Knowing Christ isn't a cheap guarantee that you can do anything you like and still spend eternity in heavenly bliss. Dabbling in astrology, palm reading, and tarot cards isn't something God ignores in His people.

Zephaniah reprimanded the people of Judah for a similar divided allegiance. He never said that they didn't give God a piece of their lives. They did—but they held on to Baal worship, too. They looked to the stars for answers as well as going to the temple.

God doesn't save a piece of your life; He saves all of it. A faithful response is to give Him your whole life in return. You can't do that if you're also trying to use occult methods to see what the future holds.

You may not know your whole future, but you know who holds it. Trust in Him.

Thank You, Lord, for holding my future. I want to trust You for everything.

∞

Many do not recognize the fact as they ought, that Satan has got men fast asleep in sin and that it is his great device to keep them so. He does not care what we do if he can do that. We may sing songs about the sweet by and by, preach sermons, and say prayers until doomsday, and he will never concern himself about us if we don't wake anybody up. But if we awake the sleeping sinner, he will gnash on us with his teeth. This is our work—to wake people up.

CATHERINE BOOTH

Day 30

Character Counts

Who can find a virtuous woman?
for her price is far above rubies.
Proverbs 31:10 kjv

When you date someone, do you look for the best-looking girl around, the guy with the most money—or a person with good character? Dreams of your future spouse probably include a great-looking person, romantic evenings together, and wonderful conversations. You may not imagine a man who's truthful or a woman who treats her parents with respect.

God doesn't say you can't marry a good-looking mate or even one with a hefty bank account, but you could live without those. You can't live happily with a weak character. Character doesn't look glamorous. You can't show off by sending your friend a picture of it. . .but you can live with it for a lifetime. You'll never worry where your mate is when you know he's trustworthy. You'll never fear a family get-together when you know she'll treat your parents kindly.

Is your date a *noble* character—or just a character?

Lord, character may not be the asset I'm dreaming of, but I know it's important. Turn my heart toward someone with a strong love for You and the willingness to do right.

You must look into people, as well as at them.

LORD CHESTERFIELD

RENEWAL

Therefore we are buried with him by baptism
into death: that like as Christ was raised up
from the dead by the glory of the Father,
even so we also should walk in newness of life.
ROMANS 6:4 KJV

You may have been a Christian for awhile, with that brand-new, clean feeling of new faith now slowly evaporating. You don't feel new anymore. *Maybe,* you ponder, *"new" is only for baby Christians. I know I've made "progress,"* you encourage yourself. *I'm not the same person I was before I knew Jesus. But something's missing.*

God didn't make Jesus new for a day, week, or month and then let Him get "old" again. He eternally raised Him from the dead, so through baptism we can share His new life forever.

If vibrant faith has left you, some "old" things probably tarnish your new life. Legalistic or critical attitudes, disobedience, and doubt take the shine off a once-new faith, until you barely know you've been changed.

But repentance during a "let's-clear-the-air" time with God returns the "new" to eternal life. Spend time with Him in prayer.

Empty me of old things that keep me apart from You, Lord. I want to spend every new day close by Your side.

✦

Do not have your concert first and then tune your instrument afterwards. Begin the day with the Word of God and prayer, and get first of all into harmony with Him.

HUDSON TAYLOR

31 Days with God
for Mothers
ISBN 978-1-60260-016-4

31 Days with God
for Grads
ISBN 978-1-60260-017-1

31 Days with God
for Fathers
ISBN 978-1-60260-018-8

ONLY 99 CENTS EACH!

AVAILABLE WHEREVER CHRISTIAN BOOKS ARE SOLD.